A STUDENT'S COMPANION
TO
PATANJALI

A Presentation of the Yoga Sutras
in the form of Questions,
Answers and Comments

by
Roger Worthington

GH00640832

THEOSOPHICAL PUBLISHING HOUSE LTD
12 Bury Place, London WC1A 2LE

Adyar, Madras
India

Wheaton, Illinois
USA

© Theosophical Publishing House Ltd., 1987
ISBN 0–7229–5064–0

Typeset by QT and Clifford Design-Associates,
Farnham, Surrey

Printed by Whitstable Litho Ltd., Whitstable, Kent

CONTENTS

FOREWORD

The widespread interest in the source literature of yoga, among students with no knowledge of Sanskrit, amply justifies this addition to the various translations of Patanjali's Yoga Sutras already available. Its title is appropriate, for its unique approach through Questions and Answers makes it a most desirable companion for both the newer and the more experienced student. Roger Worthington places himself in the position of one who is approaching the guru in order to learn from him the rationale and the techniques of yoga practice. Treating Patanjali's text as the guru's answers, he has imagined what the student's questions might have been and has formulated them in clear and straightforward language. In so doing, he identifies himself with today's learner who, with the help of the suggested questions, is thus enabled to grasp more fully the essence of the instruction.

The method has further advantage; as question and answers follow one another in a continuous flow of thought, the student will find he is able to make a preliminary reading of Patanjali's condensed statements from beginning to end and thus to glimpse an overall view of the course of instruction on which he is about to embark. In this he is further assisted by the translater's decision to place the explanatory notes, brief but adequate, at the end of each chapter where, without interrupting the chain of thought, they are readily accessible when required to elucidate points of difficulty.

The addition of an Index of all key terms, as well as a Glossary, ensures that this version of the Sutras will remain a valuable aid for students of Patanjali through many years of study: truly, a good companion.

Ianthe H. Hoskins

PREFACE

As I begin some preliminary explanation of the text, I am aware of not wanting to write *about* yoga. Much has been written about yoga and it is not my intention to add to that; nonetheless, a few words of explanation are necessary to acquaint the reader with the book and enable him to derive the most from its study. It is study that will be needed, for reading a book such as this with the eye and not the mind will be unproductive and may leave the reader more baffled than informed.

As to why this came to be written – the idea came from Miss Ianthe Hoskins who, besides introducing me to the subject of yoga some years ago, continues to offer help and encouragement, and to her I record my thanks. I also extend my thanks to Miss Jeanine Miller, whose kindness in checking the manuscript is greatly appreciated. There appears to be no other work which approaches the subject of the Yoga Sutras in the form of question and answer; it was being aware of this gap that led to the writing of this book, and it is hoped that it will appeal both to the first time reader as well as to the experienced student. The translation has been made from the Sanskrit.

Question and answer is an old established method of teaching, and one can well imagine that these sutras or aphorisms were given by Patanjali in answer to questions put to him by his students or followers. The brevity of the sutras was an aid to memory, and they represent a codification of the teachings of yoga which would have been known to Patanjali. The science of yoga is one of the oldest sciences and Patanjali, though not the originator of these teachings, was the first to expound them systematically.

There are many schools or disciplines of yoga, only some of which are familiar to us in the West. Raja Yoga, which is the subject of these sutras, is the Yoga of Will. It is a synthesis of various disciplines and takes elements from each of the schools. It is essentially a spiritual discipline, not a physical one, the control and understanding of the mind being the central themes.

Patanjali divides the text into four sections or Books, and the numbered sutras are the text. The questions are my own, as are the notes, which are intended to clarify the text rather than to provide a full commentary. Where a phrase is in brackets in the text, it has been added in order to "complete" the sutra, for often the sutras are so condensed as not to form a sentence at all. The retention of Sanskrit has been kept to a minimum, but Sanskrit cannot be avoided altogether because many words are not capable of precise translation. Sanskrit is to the philosophy of yoga rather as Italian is to the study of music, i.e. one cannot know a great deal about either without knowing something of the appropriate language. Sanskrit words that have been retained are explained briefly in the Glossary, together with their exact spelling in transliteration. An index based on these words has been added to facilitate cross-referencing.

The four Books do not need to be studied in order; Book Two is the most practical in that it deals with preliminary yoga and covers the first five of the Eight Limbs or steps of yoga; Book Three covers the remaining three steps and describes the results of becoming accomplished in the techniques of meditation. Books One and Four describe the purpose of yoga, the goal of Liberation, the various types of meditation and the transformations of the mind.

Karma, the relationship between the material and spiritual

worlds and between Nature and the Soul, the causes of sorrow, the nature of mind – these are some of the subjects discussed in the Yoga Sutras. Their profound significance may be appreciated by the reader, and in this short text enough material is contained to guide him through years or lifetimes of study and practice, even to the attainment of the goal of Liberation.

R.W. 1987

BOOK ONE – MEDITATION

1. Now, let us begin an exposition of yoga.

Q. How may yoga be defined?

2. Yoga is the process by which the mind is controlled through the transformation of the thinking principle.   *Note 1*

Q. What results from this control of the mind?

3. At these times of concentration the Seer is united with his own True Self.

Q. What is the state of consciousness at other times?

4. The Seer then identifies with the ordinary content of the mind.

Q. How does the mind function in its normal state?

5/6. Its modifications are fivefold and some cause pain while others do not. They are as follows: Right Knowledge; Wrong Knowledge; Imagination; Sleep and Memory.

Q. How are the modifications explained?   *Note 2*

7. Right Knowledge may be acquired by direct perception (from first hand experience), by deduction (based on previous experience) or by testimony (from one who knows the truth).

8. Wrong Knowledge is an idea which does not correspond with the truth.

9. Imagination is the formation of ideas which have no objective existence.

10. In Sleep there is an absence of conscious mental activity.

11. Memory is the recollection of past experiences to the present state of mind.

Q. How does one control these states of mind?

12. Control is to be gained by persistent practice and non-attachment.

Q. What does this entail?

13. Persistent practice means regularity of effort and concentration (on the chosen ideal).

14. This practice becomes rooted by application over a long period, without interruption and in a spirit of devotion.

15. Non-attachment is achieved by the perfect mastery over desires for objects that are seen and heard (gross and subtle).

Q. What state is achieved by this practice?

16. The highest state of detachment (vairagya) comes from an awareness of the Self (or the purusha) and the renunciation of the desire for the characteristic properties of matter (the gunas).   *Note 3*

Q. How can conscious illumination be experienced?   *Note 4*

17. Conscious illumination is achieved in four stages, by reasoning, reflection, bliss and pure sense of being.

Q. How can the illumination be described which is without full consciousness?

18. In this case, the content of the mind (pratyaya) is dropped, leaving only the remnant impression (samskara) after previous practice (of the particular samadhi described in I 17).   *Note 5*

Q. What are the requirements for the accomplishment of samadhi?

19. Birth can be the cause of illumination in the case of those who became merged with prakriti (Nature) in a previous incarnation.

20. In others faith, energy, memory and deep understanding must precede the attainment of samadhi.

21. Success will be more immediate with intensity of effort.

22. Progress will be determined by the mild, moderate or intense degree of effort applied.

23. Resignation of the self to Ishvara (will also bring illumination). *Note 6*

Q. How can Ishvara be described?

24. Ishvara is a particular purusha untouched by misery, karma, or even the impressions of desires. *Note 7*

25. In Him, Omniscience is unsurpassed.

26. Being beyond limitation, He is teacher even of the teachers who have gone before. *Note 8*

27. His designator is the humming sound (or sacred syllable OM).

Q. How can the consciousness of the individual find identification with Ishvara?

28. By constant repetition of the sound (OM) and by meditation on its meaning. *Note 9*

29. Then is the turning inward of consciousness and the removal of obstacles achieved.

Q. What are these obstacles which cause distraction of the mind?

30. The nine obstacles are disease, langour, doubt, carelessness, laziness, hankering after objects, delusion, inability to maintain progress and unsteadiness of mind.

Q. What are the symptoms of a distracted state of mind?

31. The symptoms are sorrow, despair, nervousness and hard breathing.

3

Q. How can these obstacles be overcome? *Note 10*

32. For the removal of obstacles there should be intense concentration on a single truth or principle.

33. Purification of the mind will result from cultivating attitudes of friendliness, compassion, delight and indifference respectively towards happiness, misery, virtue and vice.

34. Exhalation and restraining of the breath is another method of purification.

35/36. Steadiness of mind will also arise from concentration upon higher sensory experience, or from concentration upon the Inner Light (or luminosity) which is beyond sorrow.

Note 11

37. Fixity of mind on those who are without attachment to earthly passions (will also cause the removal of obstacles).

38/39. Other methods are the recollection of experiences in the dream state or in dreamless sleep, and the practice of meditation on any chosen object or ideal. *Note 12*

Q. What ultimately is achieved when the mind is thus unobstructed?

40/41. Perfect mastery extending from the finest atom to the greatest infinity results; also a state of fusion between the cogniser, cognition and the cognised, in which the mind acts like a transparent jewel. *Note 13*

Q. Can the different types of samadhi be more fully explained?

42. The samadhi that is characterised by reasoning allows the mind to alternate between different types of knowledge, i.e. that which is based on words, that which relates to objects and that which is derived from meditation.

43. The samadhi that transcends reasoning (by the intellect alone) comes with the clarification of memory, when the true

4

knowledge of an object is comprehended, without self-awareness.

44/45. The subtler stages of meditation which follow are experienced in the same way (with or without self-awareness). The objects of meditation here include everything up to the subtlest types of matter, which are without distinction.

Note 14

46. These types of samadhi are called sabija samadhi, or meditation with 'seed'.

Q. When sabija samadhi has been accomplished, what can be said then of the mental state?

47/48. When the mind has been steadied by the practice of samadhi without reasoning (and subjectivity), the clear light of spirituality begins to shine and the mind is pervaded by true knowledge and understanding. *Note 15*

Q. What is the difference between knowledge gained in samadhi and that acquired by the intellect alone?

49. True knowledge obtained in the higher states of consciousness is not confined to a particular object, unlike ordinary knowledge based on inference and testimony.

Q. Can impressions (either now or from the memory) be prevented from entering the mind and causing distractions?

50. The impression produced in the mind by the practice of sabija samadhi (meditation with seed) is strong enough to obstruct all others.

Q. What lies beyond the accomplishment of this type of samadhi?

51. When even the modifications of the mind which arise from sabija samadhi have been overcome, then follows that which is 'seedless', or nirbija samadhi. *Note 16*

NOTES ON BOOK ONE

1. It is essential to understand this definition of yoga. The student will notice that it is the mental plane, and not the physical, with which we are concerned. The phrase "thinking principle" is used because we are not talking about a particular mind as belonging to any individual, but about the universal principle of Mind, or manas; it is the function of yoga to control the workings of the mind by the application of the disciplines described. When the mind is controlled, it can perform its true function as an instrument of communication between the higher spiritual Self, or atman, and the individual personality or lower self. Yoga is thus a turning inward to find and become re-united with the true permanent Self, whose very existence is normally veiled from our consciousness by the illusions which we see as truths, as a result of our state of ignorance, or avidya.   Cf.I 2

2. The modifications of the mind are the various types of mental activity which occur in normal waking consciousness.
                                                                    I 7–11

3. Terms such as these (given in brackets) are worth remembering because firstly, they have no easy equivalent in English, and secondly, they occur frequently in studying the philosophy of yoga. All Sanskrit terms used are listed in the Glossary.   I 16

4. This sutra is concerned with a type of samadhi know as samprajnata samadhi, which is an exalted state of meditation on an object or idea experienced knowingly, i.e., in full waking consciousness.   I 17

5. This sutra clearly accompanies I 17 in explaining the next type of samadhi, called asamprajnata samadhi, in which

consciousness of the intelligent mind is transcended in a state of Self-awareness (or union with the Divine within); however, memory of previous experience in samadhi is retained in this higher state of illumination.   I 18

6.   Following the path of devotion is another and shorter method of achieving the goal of illumination, or liberation, for in exceptional cases the yogi achieves union without going through all the procedures outlined in Book Two. He is unlikely to be successful if the vehicles of the mind, body and emotions are untrained, but it is a high state of spirituality that is sought, not the practice of observances and disciplines for their own sake.   I 23

7.   On account of his references to Ishvara, Patanjali is sometimes considered theistic in his philosophy. I am inclined to think it is not of great significance whether or not this label is used, for in referring to the ruler of our Solar System, Patanjali is not entering into a debate on metaphysics, nor is he trying to limit the indefinable by attaching attributes to his conception of a Supreme Being. It should be understood that the yogic ideal is one of Self-realisation and leaves no room for dependence on any personal deity.   I 23–26

8.   Here we find reference to the timelessness of the 'Ancients', the great spiritual Teachers of the past.   I 26

9.   OM, sometimes written AUM, is the Sacred Mantra the meaning of which will come to be understood only through the practice of meditation. The essence of the three phases of manifestation and the three modes of consciousness is contained within the meaning of the word AUM. This relates to the downward process of involution, whereas the essence of OM which is breath relates to the upward spiral of spiritual evolution. OM is indivisible and has the power to transcend the world of manifestation; the utterance of the Sacred

7

Syllable (or pranava) is therefore of great significance, especially to one who is Illumined. I 28

10.   I 32-39 list various methods and practices for the training of the mind.

11.   It is almost a matter of conjecture what Patanjali is describing here, for there is a wide difference of opinion between the various translators. It would seem that this higher sensory experience is a refinement of the ordinary physical senses that results from a specific type of meditation. The Inner Light, or luminosity, is a reference to the feeling of spiritual well-being, when all the vehicles are working in perfect harmony; this experience of inner peace will bring all modifications of the mind to a halt during meditation and so strengthen control of the mind in ordinary waking consciousness. I 35, 36

12.   This last suggestion leaves the field wide open, and from it we may conclude that if the method is right and is pursued in the right spirit, it is likely to meet with success. I 39

13.   These sutras are of great significance for, as Patanjali is at pains to point out, there is no limit to the knowledge and understanding of the yogi accomplished in the techniques of samadhi. The state of union which results from the continued practice of these techniques brings the destruction of the artificial barriers which we erect between the consciousness of the individual and the object of his attention, as Seer and Seen become one. In this state the mind no longer allows its own character to influence or to colour that which is being perceived, for the person who is the knower also performs the act of knowing, without being separated from that which is known. Thus a state of fusion is said to exist without interference from the rational mind. I 40, 41

14.   These different types of samadhi require a little explanation. I 42 and 43 are contrasting the samadhi that allows the mind to function in full self-awareness and the samadhi that goes beyond the normal functions of the mind. The highest state of illumination has to leave thought behind, because thought, being an attribute of mind, is conditioned and limited by all types of experience; in the Shiva Sutras (I 17) one reads that "knowledge of the atman is gained by suspending the normal processes of the mind". If the highest state of meditation were to be described as the union of the higher, spiritual Self and the Universal Consciousness, then no thought of any kind can be present in samadhi. All thought activity must relate to individual consciousness, even if devoid of self-interest.

Concerning the objects of meditation in this type of samadhi, we need to look ahead to II 18 and 19 where Patanjali is describing the nature of the Seen and its characteristic properties. All objects can be described in relation to one or more of the three gunas (cf. II *Note* 7) which are themselves divided into four categories or stages. It is to these stages that reference is made in the text of I 45. Meditation which is without an object (i.e. "seedless") comes when self-interest and self-awareness cease and only the luminosity of Spiritual Union, which is Pure Bliss, remains.

These sutras elaborate what was given in I 17 of the yoga sutras.   I 42-45

15.   This type of knowledge involves awakening the faculty of intuition.   I 48

16.   In this state of "seedless" meditation (i.e. meditation that is not based on an object), Self-realisation, or awareness of the true nature of consciousness, is experienced (cf. I 3).   I 51

9

BOOK TWO – THE PRACTICE OF YOGA

Q. What are the preliminary steps of yoga?

1. A disciplined life, self-study and one-pointed dedication to Ishvara constitute preliminary yoga practice.   *Note 1*

Q. What is the purpose of this preliminary yoga?

2. To wear down the causes of sorrow and to attain samadhi.

Q. What are the causes of sorrow?

3. Ignorance, which is to mistake the unreal for the real; the sense of I-am-ness (being conscious only of one's own personality); attachment to experiences that are pleasurable and repulsion from those which are not; the thirst for life (and repeated experience on the physical plane); these are the causes of sorrow (or kleshas) which are at the root of all suffering.

4/5. Ignorance (avidya) is the source of the other kleshas, whether they are in a dormant, attenuated or active state. Avidya is mistaking the non-eternal, the impure, the sorrowful and the non-spirit for their opposites.   *Note 2*

6. The sense of I-am-ness is the identification of consciousness with the power of perception.   *Note 3*

7/8. Attachment arises from pleasurable experience; repulsion arises from that which results in pain or sorrow.

9. Even the wise may be dominated by the thirst for life and fear of death.   *Note 4*

Q. What is the best way of dealing with these causes of sorrow?

10. When reduced to their subtle form, they can each be resolved back to their cause or origin.   *Note 5*

11. Control of their outward form may be gained through meditation.

Q. How is karma related to the subject of the kleshas (or causes of sorrow)?

12/13. The store of karma which is rooted in the kleshas will bring all kinds of experience either in this life or in future lives. As long as the root remains, it must come to fruition in accordance with the laws of cause and effect.   *Note 6*

Q. What will be the nature of these experiences?

14. They will be pleasurable or painful according to their origins being in virtue or vice.

Q. What is the effect of these experiences upon the mind?

15. Change, anxiety and mental impressions cause sorrow and conflict, even with the wise, on account of the modifications of the mind and the workings of the gunas (or characteristic properties of matter).   *Note 7*

Q. Can one do anything about the karma which is yet to come?

16/17. Future suffering should be avoided by right living in the present; the cause of this suffering may be found in the false identification between the Seer and the Seen.

Q. What is the nature of the objective world?

18. It, the Seen, consists of the elements and sense-organs and is known by the characteristics of cognition, activity and stability; its purpose is (for individual consciousness) to gain experience of, and freedom from, the world of matter.   *Note 8*

19. They (the three gunas) have four stages of development: the particular, the universal, the differentiated and the

undifferentiated. *Note 9*

Q. What then is the nature of the Seer?

20. The Seer is pure consciousness but appears otherwise on account of its seeing through the content of the mind (which obscures the clarity of vision). *Note 10*

Q. What is the purpose of the Seen?

21. The Seen exists purely for the sake of the Seer. *Note 11*

22. It, the Seen, becomes dead to him whose purpose has been fulfilled, but remains alive to others who share the same field of experience (but have not yet reached their goal).

23. The Seer and the Seen come together for the purusha to gain experience and to come to know its own true nature. *Note 12*

24. Ignorance is the cause of this coming together (or, the lack of awareness by the purusha of its own true nature).

Q. How can this association be broken?

25. The dispelling of ignorance destroys the illusion that the Seer and the Seen are the same; this remedy leads to the liberation of the Seer. *Note 13*

26. Continuous discrimination between the Self and the not-Self is the remedy for the dispelling of ignorance.

Q. Following the dispelling of ignorance, how is enlightenment achieved?

27/28. Conscious enlightenment is achieved in seven stages. First comes the destruction of impurity after practice of the component exercises of yoga; then will arise spiritual knowledge and discrimination.

Q. What are the component exercises of yoga?

29. Self-restraints (yama), fixed observances (niyama), postures (asanas), control of the breath (pranayama), abstrac-

tion (pratyahara), concentration (dharana), meditation (dhyana) and illumination (samadhi) form the Eight Limbs of Yoga.

Q. What are the self-restraints?

30. The self-restraints are non-violence, non-falsehood, non-stealing, non-sensuality and non-acquisitiveness.   *Note 14*

31. Together they constitute the Great Vow and are not limited by time, place or circumstance. They apply to all stages (of development).

Q. What are the fixed observances?

32. The fixed observances are purity, contentment, self-discipline, self-study and surrender of the self to the Divine.

Q. How is one to tackle the problem of impure thoughts arising in the mind?

33/34. Dwelling on the opposites is the way to overcome impure thoughts and emotions. Endless misery and ignorance may result if they remain unchecked, causing suffering to oneself and to others. These impurities might be the result of greed, anger or delusion, and be of mild, medium or intense degree.

Q. What results from the continued practice of yama and niyama (the ten fixed observances)?

35. All enmities will cease in the presence of one who is firmly established in non-violence.

36. An understanding of action and reaction will result from being firmly established in truthfulness.   *Note 15*

37. Wealth comes to one who is established in honesty.
Note 16

38. Energy is conserved by the practice of non-sensuality.

39. Knowledge of the causes of existence will come to one who is rooted in non-acquisitiveness (or one who is free from

greed). *Note 17*

40. Dislike of the physical body and disinclination for physical contact with others arise from the habit of cleanliness (or physical purity).

41. Inner purity, cheerfulness of mind, one-pointedness, mastery of the senses and a fitness for the realisation of the Self arise from the habit of mental purity.

42. Supreme happiness flows from contentment.

43. Perfection of the body and senses follow the destruction of impurities by means of self-discipline. *Note 18*

44. Spiritual union with the chosen deity arises from self-study. *Note 19*

45. The attainment of samadhi comes from the surrender of the self to the Divine. *Note 20*

Q. By what method may the asanas (postures) be perfected?

46. Posture should always be steady and comfortable.

47. Perfect posture comes from relaxation of effort and meditation on the Infinite. *Note 21*

Q. What results from the continued practice of the asanas (postures)?

48. One is then no longer assaulted by the pairs of opposites. *Note 22*

Q. How can pranayama, the next of the Eight Limbs of Yoga, be perfected?

49. This stage constitutes control of the inhalation and exhalation of vital energy (pranayama).

50. Control may be external or internal and may involve the suspension of the breath; it will vary in place, time and number and may be prolonged or brief.

51. There is a fourth stage of control concerning the whole

range of internal and external breath. *Note 23*

Q. What results from the continued practice of pranayama (or the control of vital energy)?

52/53. The covering of the Inner Light is thus removed and the mind becomes fit for concentration (dharana). *Note 24*

Q. What is the next stage of yoga?

54. Abstraction (pratyahara) is where the sense organs are withdrawn from their objects in response to control by the mind.

Q. What results from the continued practice of pratyahara (abstraction)?

55. Complete mastery over the senses is then achieved.

NOTES ON BOOK TWO

1. These steps are collectively termed Kriya Yoga. The third step requires some comment: dedication to Ishvara does not mean worshipping any divine agency or personal god; rather it implies the complete resignation of the personal self to the highest imaginable ideal. In this way all one's thoughts and actions are given purpose and the life of the individual becomes focused on and directed towards the attainment of this ideal (cf. I 23).   II 1

2. Ignorance, therefore, is the incorrect perception of life as seen through the clouded senses.   II 4, 5

3. It is easy to mistake the personal self and the power of perception which belongs to the mind for our own inner consciousness, which is the true Seer. That which is perceived in the mind has the appearance of reality, but true Self-consciousness is not the same, and it is easy for the individual to be deceived into thinking "I am this" or "I am that".

   The individuality which comprises the thinking mind, the body and the senses is only temporary and is always subject to the power of illusion. Discrimination has to be employed to make a distinction between this personal self and the real Self which Is, but which can neither act nor think (cf. II 25, 26). This Self is the Seer which is often confused with the personality or individuality and which dominates the mind in ordinary waking consciousness (cf. II 21).   II 6

4. The thirst for life accompanied by the fear of death is a sign of attachment to life on the physical plane. These impulses, which may be instinctive, show desire for repeated experience and bring satisfaction to the personality through the senses, the emotions or the mind. All this, however,

creates a barrier to the attainment of samadhi. II 9

5.   This sutra underlines the practical nature of the work in hand. The instructions are quite specific for dealing with the causes of sorrow which affect us all; it is a characteristic of the discipline of yoga that the individual has to learn to trace outward manifestations back to their inward cause, i.e., to tackle a problem at its root. II 10

6.   Patanjali here is illustrating the principle which in biblical terms can be described by saying "whatsoever ye sow, that shall ye surely reap". In other words, the cause of our present sorrow may be non-evident or belong to a previous incarnation, and likewise, our present actions may be the cause of future suffering. However, if the laws of Nature are broken in any way, equilibrium must be restored, according to the laws of karma. The manner in which this takes place will vary, however, and may not accord with our ordinary notions of justice. II 12, 13

7.   Present happiness and pleasure will often end in sorrow and suffering because the very basis of these experiences is illusory and temporary. Lasting happiness and contentment are spiritual in origin; therefore they are not subject to passing moods and can never be taken away. The potentiality of the opposites always exists, i.e., one experience or sensation invariably implies its opposite. Just as in Nature lightness turns to darkness and heat gives way to cold, so in the realm of human experience, happiness gives way to sorrow and hope may lead to despair. These opposites are inherent one in the other and both sides must be experienced before consciousness can be free from domination by the senses and emotions. As the yogi does not choose to dwell on pleasurable experience, neither will he be downcast by the experience of suffering.
II 15

8. It is impossible for the individual consciousness to be freed from something which has not first been experienced. In other words, it (the purusha) cannot be aware of its own inherent spirituality unless it has known first the pain of separation by being immersed in the phenomenal world of matter. In the course of this immersion, knowledge is slowly gained which enables progress to be made; the purusha may thus come to know its own true nature (cf. II 23). II 18

9. These three gunas in their various states constitute every aspect of the phenomenal world; the four states listed here correspond with the four states of consciousness listed in I 17, i.e., reasoning – the particular; reflection – the universal; bliss – the differentiated; and pure sense of being – the undifferentiated.

This is a somewhat technical area in yogic philosophy, but the method of categorising states and types of matter in this way is scientific and should be appreciated by the modern analytical mind. Several different words are used by various translators and commentators, but the three gunas may be understood as equilibrium (sattva), activity (rajas) and inertia (tamas); anything belonging to the objective world of manifestation is said to be characterised by one of these three states. II 19

10. If, however, the mind can be brought under the control of the Higher Self (or atman), purity and clarity of vision arises. Consciousness (or purusha) is then able to perceive the truth without obstruction arising from mental impressions.

II 20

11. What is implied here is that prakriti (the Seen, or Nature) has no objective existence of its own; its function is to help fulfil the purposes of the purusha (the Seer, or Pure Consciousness). II 21

12. This sutra is central to the understanding of Book Two or, one could say, of the whole philosophy of yoga, since it describes the very cause of man's physical existence and begins to answer the question "well, what is one doing here anyway?"   II 23

13. This distinction between the Seer (purusha, which is permanent) and the Seen (prakriti, which is subject to both change and decay) needs to be understood. Ignorance arises when the Seer mistakenly identifies himself with the Seen and prevents the personality from coming to know its own Inner Self. The liberation of the Seer is possible only when this barrier has been removed.

It might be useful at this point to draw a distinction between the terms purusha and atman. Purusha is used in the present context because it refers to the Inner Self or the Seer, whereas atman is the spirit of Universal Consciousness, known in Hindu philosophy as Brahman. In the Upanishads and in the Viveka Chudamani (by Shri Shankaracharya, thought to be a pupil of Patanjali), atman and Brahman are many times equated with one another. Atman is changeless and unaffected by the action of the individual; it is always present whether or not one is aware of its presence. Purusha on the other hand, although permanent, evolves through contact with prakriti, which is the objective world or Nature. To use a different terminology, atman may simply be described as the Spirit and purusha the Soul.   II 25

14. The five vows or self-restraints are generally expressed in negative terms; they may be understood, however, as harmlessness, truthfulness, honesty, temperance and freedom from greed.

Their interpretation and application are a matter for the individual to decide; by way of indication, non-violence should extend towards the animal kingdom, which is as much a part of Nature as man; non-falsehood includes the subtler forms of deception which tend to go unnoticed; non-stealing includes misappropriation of any kind, requiring compliance with the highest moral codes of behaviour; non-sensuality does not have to mean sexual abstinence, but rather temperance and moderation, always behaving within the bounds of morality; non-acquisitiveness is meant in both the material and spiritual sense of not seeking possessions, honours or rewards for their own sake, and holding lightly to those things which may be in one's possession. To observe these laws is to comply with the laws of Nature, thereby conserving vital energy and bringing tranquillity of mind.   II 30

15.   This sutra needs a little amplification. Some translators speak of the yogi attaining power to bring about the fruits of action without performing the action itself. This idea does not seem to come from the text; however, what would seem to be implied is that an understanding of the real connection between cause and effect, or action and reaction, arises from being rooted in non-falsehood.   II 36

16.   Differences of opinion also arise over the translation of this sutra; an alternative translation could be that "one who is firmly established in non-stealing is in no way distracted by gems and precious stones put before him"; in other words, true wealth is a state of spirituality and has nothing to do with possessions and their accumulation.   II 37

17.   Greed and acquisitiveness cause the mind to be focused on material things, which prevent it from functioning at the intuitive level where more profound knowledge of birth and existence is to be found.   II 39

18.   In this sutra the root cause of the development of the siddhis (psychic powers) such as clairvoyance and clairaudience

is revealed. Many of the sutras in Book Three are given over to a detailed account of these siddhis; it could be added, however, that these powers are not to be treated as objects of pursuit, for they come unbidden, we are told, to those who have fulfilled the conditions. II 43

19.   If the mind of the individual becomes focused on a particular image or concept, after a time it will become identified with that concept; in the case of a deity or object of devotion, the perceiver may become merged with the object of perception. When the mind is thus focused, it can act "like a transparent jewel", being free from all impurities (cf. I 40, 41). If the object of perception is the product of thought and created in the image of man, delusion will result, but if self-study is directed inwards to the atman (or centre of consciousness), then knowledge of the Inner Self will result and the consciousness of the individual will become merged with the Divine within. II 44

20.   This reaffirms what was said in I 23. In other words, the fixed observance of "surrender of the self to the Divine" is also an essential part of preliminary or kriya yoga (cf. II 1).

II 45

21.   Both mind and body must be controlled before successful posture is achieved; with relaxation of effort, there should be no struggle in performing the asanas. Any struggle would defeat the purpose of the exercise and be more likely to create tension than prepare the mind and body for the state of samadhi. II 47

22.   Accomplishment of the postures by control of the mind and body should leave one free from the effects of the opposites, such as heat and cold, which can otherwise dominate the mind. II 48

23.   These sutras are of a technical nature and their exact

21

meaning is obscure; the various translations differ considerably and it is likely that their content can be fully understood only by becoming fully accomplished in the practice of pranayama oneself.   II 50, 51

24.   The use of the word Light here requires some comment. The "light within" is normally obscured by a lack of purity, so that the light which emanates from the subtle vehicles (and which is visible to the inner sight of the yogi) cannot shine. When the obstacles are removed, not only can the Inner Light shine, but also the consciousness of the yogi is thus prepared for the practice of dharana (from which will result the light of understanding). The purification of the subtle bodies, therefore, is the main purpose behind the practice of pranayama.
                                                            II 52, 53

BOOK THREE – THE BOOK OF POWERS

Q. What are the last three limbs of yoga?

1. The first is concentration (dharana), which is the fixing of the mind on a particular point.

2. The second is meditation (dhyana), in which the content of the mind is wholly absorbed in the one area.

3. Then follows illumination (samadhi), in which the mind is unaware of its own identity, being conscious only of the true nature of the chosen object.   *Note 1*

4. The three taken together are called samyama.

Q. What results from the continued practice of samyama?

5. Mastery of samyama causes the vision that is wisdom.

Q. How should it be applied?

6. Samyama is to be applied in stages.

Q. What is the nature of this threefold discipline?

7/8. The three stages are internal in relation to the earlier disciplines, but even this (samyama) is external compared with samadhi without "seed".   *Note 2*

Q. How are the transformations of the mind accomplished in passing from one state to the next?

9. Transformation from one state to another occurs when thought is momentarily suppressed between one impression leaving and another one entering the mind; the mind becomes pervaded by this moment of transformation.

10. When control is established, then the flow from one state to another is undisturbed.

Q. What other types of transformation are there?

11. The samadhi transformation arises from the weakening of distracting thoughts and the strengthening of one-pointedness in the mind.

12. A further transformation occurs when a thought which arises is exactly similar to the one that precedes, and the mind is then balanced between the movements of distraction and restraint.   *Note 3*

Q. How do these relate to the functioning of the elements and sense-organs?

13. These transformations also apply to the elements and sense-organs, which (being an extension of the principle of mind) similarly undergo changes of state, character and condition.

14. The elements (bhutas) belong to a substratum in which the properties, whether latent, manifested or yet to be manifest inhere.   *Note 4*

Q. What results from these transformations?

15. The different transformations cause differences in the natural progression of evolution.   *Note 5*

Q. What is the result of performing samyama on these three transformations?

16. Knowledge of the past and of the future results from the practice of samyama on the three transformations.

Q. What is the result of performing samyama on the concept of sound?

17. Understanding of the sounds uttered by all living beings results from the practice of samyama on the distinction between sound itself, its purpose, and the idea embodied in the sound; these otherwise occur simultaneously in a confused state.

Q. Can samyama be applied to reveal the secrets of past lives?

18. By direct perception of the impressions (retained from past lives), knowledge of previous births is revealed.   *Note 6*

Q. Can the minds of others also be understood by this practice?

19. Knowledge of the minds of others arises from direct perception of the content of the mind of another.   *Note 7*

20. Perception of the state of mind through samyama on another is not intended to reveal the thoughts and motivations which support (that state of mind).

Q. How is it possible to render the body of the yogi invisible?

21. By the application of samyama to the form of the body it is possible to suspend the powers of perception, causing the eye to be unreceptive to the movement of light (emitted by the body of the yogi); the body is then invisible.

Q. Can the other sensations be similarly affected?

22. *Sounds and other sensations can be made to disappear by the application of the same technique.   *Note 8*

(This sutra is sometimes omitted, in which case numbering for the remainder of Book Three will be different.)

Q. What results from the application of samyama to the various types of karma?

23. Knowledge of the time of death arises from the practice of samyama on karma that is active and that which is latent, or from the recognition of omens and portents.

Q. What results from the application of samyama to the human qualities?

24. Moral strength is gained by the application of samyama to (such qualities as) friendship.

Q. What results if samyama is applied to the idea of strength?

25. By the application of samyama to great strength, such as that of an elephant, super-physical strength will arise.

Note 9

Q. Is it possible to gain knowledge of things that are beyond ordinary physical perception?

26. Knowledge of the subtle, the hidden and the remote may be gained by focusing the light of perception (on a particular object).

Q. Can samyama be applied therefore to understanding the workings of the universe itself?

27. Knowledge of the worlds (or solar system) arises from the application of samyama to the sun.

28/29. From its application to the moon arises knowledge of the arrangement of the stars (or stellar system); also, knowledge of their motion can be gained from the application of samyama to the Pole star

Note 10

Q. What results from the application of samyama to parts of the human body?

30. Knowledge of the constitution of the body arises from the application of samyama to the navel chakra.

Note 11

31. Cessation of hunger and thirst arises from its application to the throat chakra.

32. Fixity of the body arises from its application to the nerve centre which forms one of the vehicles of prana.

33. Sight of perfected beings arises from its application to the light which shines within the head.

Note 12

Q. Is there any other means by which such knowledge can be gained than by the application of samyama?

34. Spiritual knowledge is also gained by direct intuitive perception.

Q. How does the intuitive faculty function with regard to the heart and the mind?

35. Knowledge of the mind arises from the application of samyama to the heart. *Note 13*

Q. What results from the application of samyama to the Self?

36. Knowledge of the purusha (Self) arises from the application of samyama to the distinction between the purusha and the sattva (or essence of matter). All kinds of experience result from the inability to distinguish between these two, the purusha (which exists for its own sake), and the sattva, which exists at the same time for others.

37. Thence (from knowledge of the purusha) arise intuitive hearing, touch, sight, taste and smell.

Q. What is the true significance of all these siddhis or powers?

38. They are obstacles in the way of samadhi, but powers when the attention is outward-turned.

Q. What other accomplishments can be attained by the aspirant on the path to perfection?

39. The mind can enter the body of another by loosening the cause of bondage and by knowledge of the channels (through which the mind centre flows). *Note 14*

40/41. Levitation and non-contact with water, mud and thorns, etc., arise from mastery over one of the vital airs, and a burning radiance from within arises from another, called udana and samana respectively (*see Glossary*).

42. Superphysical hearing arises from the practice of samyama on the relation between the ear and space (akasha). *Note 15*

43. The capacity to pass through space arises from the application of samyama to the relation between the body and

space; also by comtemplation on objects of the lightness of cotton-fibre. *Note 16*

44. Concentration on the state of mind that is unaware of, and external to the person (of the yogi), causes the covering of the light (of Universal Mind) to disappear. *Note 17*

45. Perfect understanding of the bhutas (elements) results from the practice of samyama on their various modes of functioning (cf. III 14).

Q. What results from this mastery over the elements?

46. Perfection of the body, freedom from obstruction by the elements, and siddhis, such as the ability to become as small as an atom, result from this mastery.

Q. What are the characteristics of the perfect body?

47. Beauty, grace, strength and great firmness characterize the perfect body.

Q. What results from the application of samyama to the sense-organs?

48. Complete mastery over the sense-organs results from the practice of samyama on their various modes of functioning. *Note 18*

49. From this mastery arises control over the very source of prakriti, the capacity to move as fast as thought and the power to engage the senses without any physical agency.

Q. From whence arise absolute mastery and perfection?

50. Supremacy and omniscience arise from the full realisation of the essential difference between sattva and purusha (cf. III 36).

Q. What is the final stage before the attainment of kaivalya?

51. The seed of bondage is destroyed by non-attachment even to that (the twin powers of supremacy and omniscience);

then follows kaivalya, or Liberation.

Q. What should be the response of the yogi when challenged to display his powers?

52. There should be neither pleasure nor pride when invited even by superior Beings to display one's powers, for there is always the possibility of a recurrence of the undesirable. *Note 19*

Q. What results from the application of samyama to the concept of time?

53. Discriminative knowledge arises from the practice of samyama on a particle of time and on the sequence of time.

54. From this knowledge is gained the ability to distinguish between objects that are naturally similar in type, characteristic and location. *Note 20*

55. This knowledge is transcendent and enables all objects and processes to be known at once, without limitation of space or time.

Q. When is the attainment of kaivalya made possible?

56. When the purusha and sattva are equal in purity, then is kaivalya (or Liberation) attained (cf. III 36, 50). Note 21

NOTES ON BOOK THREE

1.   These last three limbs of yoga are concerned with the specific task of developing the mind on the higher planes. They are not concerned with pure knowledge, which is an attribute of intelligence, but with intuition and spiritual awareness, which are accompanied by wisdom. The three stages are collectively termed samyama; the only English word that comes near the meaning is meditation, but this word can be taken to mean different things. Meditation has been used already to describe the seventh of the eight limbs, dhyana (cf. II 29), which is termed the second stage of samyama. However, samyama which describes the whole process of meditation cannot be too narrowly defined.

The first five limbs are really a preparation for the final three stages. Training does not have to be step-by-step or one limb at a time; it can be commenced on various levels or with various disciplines at the same time, although Patanjali describes them in order (vid. *Raja Yoga* by V.W. Slater).

Concentration, meditation and illumination are the very essence of yoga, of Raja Yoga in particular, and the technique which is outlined for their application is aimed at fulfilling the purpose of yoga described in I 2. This threefold discipline is central to the whole subject of yoga. What follows in Book Three is a description of the various powers or faculties which may be developed in the course of the continued practice of samyama. Nonetheless, possession of psychic powers is by itself no indication of the spiritual development of the individual; the siddhis are not to be regarded as objects of attainment.

The state of dharana (the first stage of samyama) has been

described as "a total catalepsy of the physical frame". From this, one can be made aware of the need for a complete transformation of consciousness before samyama can be applied at all. Mastery of samyama therefore indicates an immense achievement.   III 1–3

2.   Patanjali has recommended the step-by-step approach to samyama, and we note in this sutra that these last three limbs are different in nature from the other five. The earlier disciplines, although directed towards training the inner self, are nonetheless external observances and, practised on their own, are not true yoga. For this the meditative techniques must additionally be employed.

With meditation that has no mental object the process is described as seedless meditation, or nirbija samadhi, and indicates a higher state of illumination than sabija samadhi, or meditation with seed (cf. I 51).   III 7, 8

3.   This group of sutras deals with the transformation of the mind from one state of consciousness to another as progress is made along the path to enlightenment. The whole area is rather technical, but what can be seen is that each stage has its own particular characteristics and that there is a method of passing from one state of consciousness to the next. The technique described involves "catching", as it were, that moment of silence between one thought and the next during meditation and expanding it, thus strengthening control of the mind and creating equilibrium, or sattva. In this state there are neither new thoughts nor old, but only "seedless" meditation, or pure attention, devoid of any object.   III 9–12

4.   The Sanskrit word bhutas is used here because the term "elements", by which it is normally translated, can mean a number of things. The bhutas are a root substance of matter

31

which, when modified by the three gunas, have objectivity in the phenomenal world, existing otherwise in their latent or potential state. Unfortunately, the word bhutas has several different applications, but it is used here to mean the five natural elements: earth, fire, water, air and ether.   III 14

5.   This is a difficult sutra; it is so condensed in form as to render its full meaning unclear. This has given rise to some very different translations: the one offered complies with the Sanskrit but needs some elucidation. That the universe functions according to natural and predictable laws has been well established, but what seems to be behind this aphorism is that when the mind has undergone these transformations it is able to exert some influence on the succession of external events. This is not unreasonable, for if the yogi has brought his own mind under control, access is then gained to higher forms of knowledge by which the processes of evolution are understood.

Therefore, if the ability to make these transformations has been mastered, it should be possible to cause things to happen by the application of the laws of Nature to a particular point or situation. This works by the complete subjugation of the personal will and by attunement to the Divine Will or power within. It has nothing to do with black magic, which is the intensification of the will for the glorification of the personal self, by whatever means.   III 15

6.   The fruits of the practice of samyama, the threefold discipline of meditation, form the subject matter of the remainder of Book Three. These are the siddhis, or powers, which arise from the accomplishment of the disciplines of yoga; reference can be found in other texts to the parallel development of consciousness and power which occurs when progress is made along the path of Self-Realisation (vid. *The*

Secret of Self-Realisation by I.K. Taimni).

Pure consciousness and power are both properties of the universal atman or "cosmic soul" which are confined to the point of non-awareness in the downward process of involution. However, as the consciousness of the individual expands in the upward spiral of evolution, so the powers of the atman unfold, as the microcosmic individuality seeks union with the macrocosmic atman to which it belongs. The power of the Divine truly lies within; what is lacking is an awareness of its existence and a willingness to give it room in place of the self-centred personality.

The threefold discipline of samyama is the essential element behind all the powers enumerated; when the technique is mastered these capacities will develop, but they are most likely to result from several lifetimes of dedicated living in pursuit of the yogic ideal.   III 18

7. The telepathic communication between one mind and another and the "reading" of minds described here are easier to comprehend if it is remembered that mind consciousness is universal and not particular. The principle of mind (chitta) is rooted in the spiritual plane and is a function of the Higher Self or atman; only the functions of the thinking, lower mind are individualised to the extent that they become an attribute of the personality. Thought is not the property of an individual, because it is only an expression of consciousness pertaining to a particular moment. However, it does have an objective existence which can be "viewed" by the yogi.   III 19

8. The purpose of this "act of disappearance" is partly to protect the person of the yogi from the idle curiosity of others and also to protect others from sights and sounds, which could be misinterpreted, from being perceived. It has long been

recognised that some knowledge is only for the few who have shown the capacity to understand, and the siddhis described here enable the yogi to perform whatever tasks are necessary out of the public gaze, without the need to retreat to a place of isolation.   III 21, 22

9.   Super-physical strength can refer to that of the elephant, since the yogi who has attained this siddhi will have a deep understanding of, and mastery over, the forces of nature. However, to the student of yoga this concept of strength may have a spiritual application for which the physical force is but a symbol, i.e., one who is accomplished in the techniques of yoga will have great inner strength, derived from the power of atman.   III 25

10.   These sutras (27–29) are illustrative of the one preceding, for a working knowledge of the whole universe clearly requires perception of the subtle, the hidden and the remote. Since perception is instant, it requires no energy; it is a better and more reliable way of obtaining knowledge than the use of reason and intellect.   III 29

11.   It is well known that the chakras are psychic centres which occur at certain key parts of the body; each one controls the organs and bodily functions that are in the vicinity of that particular chakra. One can imagine therefore that, by directing one's attention exclusively to one of these centres, a definite result would occur.   III 30

12.   The "perfected beings" described here are the adepts or mahatmas who have followed the path of yoga to its goal and attained kaivalya, or liberation from the causes of bondage. The yogi lives principally on the spiritual planes, while ordinary men are usually pre-occupied with the physical and material planes of existence. For this reason adepts or

mahatmas are not normally seen in physical form.

The light to which Patanjali refers is that spiritual luminosity, or Inner Light which emanates from the crown of the head.

III 33

13. It might be useful to amplify what is meant by the words mind and heart: the former (chitta) refers to the universal mind-principle and is nothing to do with the physical functions of the brain (cf. III 7); the latter (hridaya) refers similarly to the spiritual heart-centre and not to the functions of the physical organ. Intuitive perception is a "soul experience" and is instantaneous; it requires neither reasoning intelligence nor sympathy with the object. This experience, however, is unlikely to occur if the heart and mind centres are not well balanced and evolved.

III 35

14. This ability to enter the mind of another is something that can be practised by those who have developed the appropriate siddhi. It is a useful means of carrying out a task (usually from a distance) with the assistance of another person with whom one is in sympathy, such as the pupil of an adept. The yogi does not cause that person to go into a trance, but rather causes him to act as an agent for a particular purpose. The yogi takes over the physical body of the other person, but exercises his own will for the completion of a particular task.

III 39

15. Space or ether (akasha) is the medium through which sound travels; therefore if the organ of hearing is properly understood in its relation to space, sounds normally undiscernible to the human ear may be heard.

III 42

16. This siddhi operates on a similar principle to the one just described, but the capacity to understand the exact relationship between the body and space enables the yogi to perform that which to the uninitiated would seem an impossible feat. This

power might be used as an alternative to the one described in III 39 to accomplish tasks away from the physical location of the body, perhaps enabling dangerous terrain to be crossed with ease; in this instance, however, the yogi stays with his own body instead of employing that of another person.

III 43

17.   The subject of this sutra cannot really be described by words alone as it concerns a state of consciousness outside the normal mind-centred experience. However, two results of this accomplishment are worth noting: one is the ability of the yogi to function on the spiritual-mental plane unencumbered by the physical body; the other is a greater wisdom brought about by the removal of the veil of ignorance (cf. II 52).   III 44

18.   In this sutra and in III 45 no attempt has been made by the compiler of this work to describe the "various modes of functioning"; they are more likely to confuse than to clarify the
main content of the sutra, as has tended to happen in some translations. Furthermore, Patanjali offers no explanation of them, nor does he make any later reference to them.   III 48

19.   Until one is totally free of attachment to the phenomenal world, even the yogi cannot count himself safe from distraction. To be freed finally from the pairs of opposites, there must be no room for pleasurable experience of any kind, for the seed of pain would still then be present (cf. III *Note* 7). Pleasure and pain are always closely related and all such emotions must be left behind before there can be a full awareness of atmic consciousness.   III 52

20.   When the word "object" is used in such a context, the meaning is not limited to gross physical objects but embraces anything which occupies the mind for more than a "particle of time". The power to discriminate between right and wrong,

between the real and the unreal, the true and the false, is the subject of this sutra, and in a sense a warning is given that sensory perception alone is not enough to distinguish between the two. III 54

21. Purusha, or the indwelling consciousness of the Self, must finally be equal in purity with sattva, the very essence of matter. The failure to distinguish between purusha and sattva has been cited in III 36 as the cause of continued existence, or continual experience in the chain of life, death and rebirth. When the yogi has come to understand each for what it is, he has gained the power to discriminate between the real and the unreal, the finite and the infinite. This state of equilibrium is what is needed to free individual consciousness from all limitations, for the attainment of spiritual freedom in kaivalya, or Final Liberation. III 56

BOOK FOUR – THE BOOK OF LIBERATION

Q. By what means are the siddhis or occult powers attained?

1. They are the result of either birth, medications, mantra, self-discipline or samadhi. *Note 1*

Q. What is the cause of transformation from one state or kind of existence to another?

2. An overflow of natural tendencies is the cause of the transformations (or parinamas) from one state of existence to another.

3. The real cause of transformation, however, is not the result of incidental causes stirring the natural tendencies, but the removal of hindrances from the flow of progression, as in farming. *Note 2*

Q. If the yogi needs to create duplicate mind-centres for the accomplishment of certain tasks, how are they originated?

4. Artificial mind-centres are essentially a product of the ego-sense or personality.

5. Their various activities are controlled by the one mind.

Q. In what way do these mind-centres differ from the natural mind?

6. The mind-centres born of meditation are untainted (by either desire or past impressions).

Q. How does the karma of the yogi differ from that of other people?

7. The karma of the yogi is neither black nor white (pure nor impure); that of others is of three types – pure, impure or mixed.

Q. When do the fruits of karma become manifest?

8. The potentiality of these three types of karma only comes to fruition when the conditions are favourable.

9. Although memory and impressions are the same in form, the succession (of cause and effect) can be interrupted by time, place and circumstance. *Note 3*

Q. How do the desires which give rise to fresh karma originate?

10. They have no beginning, because the will to live is eternal.

Q. How is one to break this chain of cause and effect?

11. When desires and their cause (which is ignorance) are overcome, then the bond between cause and effect and the vitality which supports the object of desire will be dispelled.

Q. How are past tendencies related to future actions?

12. Past and present exist in reality, but differences of state and condition (or dharma) result from different paths (being followed).

13. These differences may be subtle or obvious depending on the nature of the guna (or characteristic properties of matter). *Note 4*

Q. Wherein lies the essence of an object?

14. The essential nature of an object is to be found in its particular transformations. *Note 5*

Q. What is the relationship between an object and the mind that perceives it?

15. The object remains the same although differences may arise (between perception and the perceived) from minds being directed in different ways.

16. An object cannot exist for one mind only, for what

would become of it when un-perceived?

17. An object is either known or not known according to the mind being coloured by it or not. *Note 6*

Q. How is it that the inner consciousness (or purusha) is aware of the perception of an object by the mind?

18. The purusha, which is lord of the mind and without transformation, knows every modification (or colouring) of the mind.

19. Because the mind itself is perceptible, it cannot be self-illumined. *Note 7*

20/21. Neither can it function as perceiver and perceived at the same time; if that were the case, there could be other minds and endless confusion of thoughts and memories.

Note 8

Q. By what means can the mind become aware of its own movements?

22. When consciousness becomes aware of its own eternal nature, that knowledge is reflected in the mind which is then able to perceive its own movements.

23. The mind becomes all knowing when coloured by the knower and the known. *Note 9*

Q. What lies behind the movements of the mind?

24. Although influenced by numerous tendencies, the mind acts in association with the purusha (and not as a separate entity). *Note 10*

Q. What results from this understanding regarding the mind?

25/26. Once the distinction has been made between the mind and the Self, all longing comes to an end; then is the mind truly inclined towards discrimination and set on liberation, or kaivalya.

Q. Is this state of mind continuous, or periodic?

27. Interruptions in this state may arise from the strength of past impressions.

Q. By what means may these disturbances be avoided?

28. The method for the removal of such obstacles is the same as that described for the kleshas (vid.II 10, 11). *Note 11*

Q. What follows the state of constant discrimination?

29. When a constant state of discrimination is attained, even with regard to spiritual knowledge, and the awareness of the Self is uninterrupted, there follows the highest samadhi which brings freedom from all dharma that obscures Reality.

30. From this samadhi arises freedom from the causes of sorrow and the bonds of karma.

31. That which is knowable to the mind is but little compared to the infinity of knowledge that arises from the removal of all veils and impurities. *Note 12*

Q. What is the relationship between matter and the purusha following the attainment of kaivalya?

32. Then, the process of the constant transformation of the gunas comes to an end, for its purpose is fulfilled.

33. The succession of moments is only apprehensible when, like the transformations, it comes to an end. *Note 13*

Q. How is the purusha re-united with the Divine Consciousness?

34. In this state of kaivalya the gunas recede to their origin, being devoid of objectivity, and the purusha, achieving its purpose, becomes established in its own real nature which is Pure Consciousness.

NOTES ON BOOK FOUR

1. Book Four begins by developing a little further the theme from the later part of Book Three and lists possible causes for the occurrence of the siddhis, or occult powers. If they are the result of *birth*, their true cause can be supposed to belong to a previous incarnation. The word *medications* is likely to refer to the use of herbal preparations for the inducement of a particular result; this is in preference to the word drug used in some translations, but which has different connotations in modern times. The power of *mantra* through the incantation of certain key words or phrases produces results which need to form a separate area of study. *Self-discipline* embraces the whole yogic practice of adherence to a particular pattern or mode of living. *Samadhi* one expects to be the cause of occult powers on account of its belonging to the threefold practice of samyama, which is the total concentration of the mind in meditation. IV 1

2. Sutras 2 and 3 concern the parinamas, or transformations from one state or kind of existence to another. They were discussed in Book III (9 – 18) with regard to the technique of accomplishment, but here in Book IV Patanjali examines the causes of transformation, i.e., having first answered the question "how", he now addresses the question of "why". There is no added ingredient or outer agency that causes these transformations; they occur naturally when the time is right and when the obstacles have been removed.

The analogy with farming is useful because the farmer does not *cause* his crops to grow, he simply allows the natural tendencies which are inherent in the seed to flow, removing obstacles such as weeds and tending the crops. The sowing and cultivation are the indirect cause of their growth, but the real cause of growth is inherent within, not applied from without. When the conditions are right, the crops will come to fruition and changes of state and condition will occur. Likewise in the human state: if no barriers are erected by the personality and consciousness is focused inward, the individuality begins to evolve and spiritual transformation will occur.　　　IV 2, 3

3.　The basic theory of karma, in which every action has both a cause and an effect, is straightforward, but problems arise when the connection between the two is non-evident. There are times when the relationship between cause and effect is clear, but in these two sutras we are told, firstly, that the consequences of past actions become manifest only when the conditions are favourable; secondly, that our recollection of an event is essentially the same as the imprint that it made on the sub-conscious; and thirdly, that the result may appear unconnected with the cause because of changes in time, place and circumstance. In other words, the link between cause and effect, action and reaction, remains until it has been dissolved by future actions when time and circumstance are right. Present suffering may appear to lack a cause and present actions may appear to be without consequence, but neither situation actually corresponds to the truth (cf. II 12 – 17). IV 8, 9

4.　The meaning of these two aphorisms hinges on two Sanskrit words, dharma and guna. Dharma is closely linked with karma and can have a number of different meanings; karma is basically action bound by the law of cause and effect, whereas dharma is more of a duty or obligation which influences behaviour. One cannot escape from karma, only cease to generate it; but with dharma there is more of the element of choice. The state and condition of each individual (spiritually speaking) is constantly changing and is never identical for any two people at the same time. According to one's development and circumstances, certain duties or opportunities will present themselves, but whether or not one responds is another matter.

In spite of both past and present existing in their own right, the differences of dharma are as numerous as the people who experience them; so it is that no two people will react in the same way to situations that appear identical. Likewise, the tendencies and inclinations of different people will cause them to pursue different paths, even if the ultimate objective of spiritual union should be common to all.

The gunas, or properties of matter which characterise all objects in the phenomenal world (cf. II 15, 19), also relate to the individual; the balance between them is constantly changing and has a direct bearing on individual dharma. If neither activity nor inertia predominates, a state of equilibrium would exist in which the quality of goodness will find expression.   IV 12, 13

5.   The transformations of the gunas are infinite and result in the various and complex forms of the manifest world; so it is that if we wish to discover the essence of an object or phenomenon we must first appreciate the exact nature of the transformation and the properties that gave rise to it. Objects are many and tranformations are many, but the essential nature of the Ultimate Reality is the Oneness which underlies all existence.   IV 14

6.   For an object to be recognised as such, it must have existence outside the mind of the perceiver; conversely, when different minds or mind-centres view any particular object, the impression that is formed will vary according to the state or condition of the perceiver. Subjective experience colours the

mind, whereas in a state of illumination this is not the case, for when there is fusion between the cogniser, cognition and the cognised, the mind acts like a transparent jewel (cf. I 41). In consciousness of a less exalted state, the mind acts like a filter, colouring its perception according to past impressions and prejudices. It makes no difference to the object, however, which way any mind is pointed at the time the object is perceived.

An object may exist and be perceptible, but unless the mind is coloured by that object, no impression will be formed; the object therefore cannot impinge on the consciousness of a mind that is not so coloured. This process of the mind being coloured by objects and experiences, although it can be transcended, is a necessary stage in the assimilation of ordinary knowledge.   IV 15 – 17

7.   It can be seen from the previous sutra that the mind and the purusha are not the same. The mind may serve as the vehicle of inner consciousness and as a link with the personality, but it is not that inner consciousness. The purusha is self-illumined on account of its being pure spirit and eternal, but since the activities of the mind are overseen by the purusha, it follows that the mind cannot be self-illumined.

IV 19

8.   These two sutras serve to explain further IV 18 and 19. Since the mind is neither dual nor self-illumined, it cannot perceive its own functions. The mind, however, is perceptible, though it is not perceived by other minds but by the purusha. If it were otherwise, confusion would reign in every mind, for the mind can only be directed in one way at any one time. Two minds means two individuals, not one mind observing itself.

IV 20, 21

9.   The mind is always coloured by the known through

everyday experience, but what is new here is that the mind is also coloured from within as the knowledge pertaining to the purusha is reflected in the mind. This ability to perceive the movements of the mind through a conscious awareness of its own eternal nature bestows an added power on the yogi who, being illumined from within, is able to comprehend all, as perceiver and perceived are united.   IV 23

10.   This sutra is of particular significance, for attention is drawn to the distinction between the mind and the animating principle or purusha. It is suggested that the mind does not exist as a separate entity, but rather is linked inextricably with the higher consciousness, which is the hidden force behind the movements of the mind. On analysis of the sutras dealing with the nature of mind and consciousness, it becomes clear that the mind does not function as a separate entity, being pulled in all directions by the tendencies that surround it and exert pressure, but that a power exists within for the purposes of which all mental activity takes place.   IV 24

11.   In order that the goal of liberation be achieved, the true nature of mind must be understood by exercising the power of discrimination between the Self and the not-Self, the eternal and the transitory. When this distinction has been made, the mind is "inclined" towards its goal, but before the goal can be achieved, all distractions from the past must be overcome. Kaivalya is not a state of ecstasy that comes and goes, but is an attainment that is absolute and irreversible. Such a state of consciousness cannot be made to suffer interruption, for such divine spirituality has left behind all distractions of every kind.
                                                                                                IV 25 – 28

12.   What is being considered in these two sutras is no less than the attainment of kaivalya itself, or the state of perfect freedom. Liberation comes when the final effort has been

made and the awareness of the Self as becomes continuous.

Kaivalya is attained when the highest samadhi has been experienced and the causes of sorrow transcended; then there is freedom from bondage to action and the fruits of action. Ordinary knowledge gained by the mind in waking consciousness becomes insignificant in comparison with that wider knowledge which belongs to the spirit and of which the yogi is now in possession.   IV 30, 31

13.   The succession of moments is a reference to the notion of time, whereby one moment appears to succeed another in the mind of the individual. The illusory nature of this succession is only known when the modifications of the mind have ceased and all life is perceived as one unbroken whole, following the attainment of kaivalya. The changes in the characteristic properties of matter have ceased because, for the individual who has attained his goal, they have lost their meaning. The very function of the material world (prakriti) is to serve the needs of the purusha (cf. III 36); now, if the individual becomes merged in the universal flame, then for that spark matter (or prakriti) has no reality, for the Oneness of all existence has been experienced.

The language of these later aphorisms is not easy, for not only do we have to face Sanskrit terms that cannot easily be translated, but also, because of the very nature of the subject, all words are quite inadequate. However, what are being described by Patanjali are certain characteristics of the state of kaivalya in which both the transformations of matter and the process of time are found to have no further meaning, for the worlds of matter and time have been transcended.   IV 32, 33

47

BIBLIOGRAPHY

TAIMNI I.K.	The Science of Yoga	Theosophical Publishing House
TAIMNI I.K.	The Secret of Self-Realisation	T.P.H.
SLATER V.W.	Raja Yoga – a simplified and practical course	T.P.H.
BAILEY A.	The Light of the Soul	Lucis
PRABHAVANANDA & ISHERWOOD	How to know God	Allen & Unwin
PUROHIT & YEATS	Aphorisms of Yoga	Faber
VIVEKANANDA	Raja Yoga	Longman
DVIVEDI	The Yoga Sutras of Patanjali	R. Tukaram, Bombay
JOHNSTON C.	The Yoga Sutras of Patanjali	John Watkins
STEPHEN D.R.	Patanjali for Western Readers	Theosophical Society
WOOD E.	Practical Yoga	Rider
VENKATESANANDA	Enlightened Living	Chiltern Yoga Trust

GLOSSARY of SANSKRIT TERMS

The spelling used here is the one commonly used in translit-eration. The spelling given in brackets is the form which will be found in a dictionary, the diacritical marks indicating the pronunciation and enabling the exact Sanskrit characters to be identified.

AKASHA [ākāśa]
  Space; the etheric fluid or universal element

ASAMPRAJNATA [asamprajñata]
  Beyond or without consciousness

ASANA [āsana]
  Posture (the third of the eight limbs of yoga)

ATMAN [ātman, sometimes written ātmā]
  Spirit or Universal Consciousness

AVIDYA [avidyā]
  Ignorance; the state of not knowing

BHUTAS [bhūtas]
  Elements (as in nature)

BRAHMAN [brahman]
  The One Universal Spirit or atman

CHAKRA [cakra]
  A psychic centre through which energy passes to particular parts of the body

CHITTA [citta]
  Consciousness; mind; the thinking principle

DHARANA [dhāraṇā]
  Concentration (one of the three stages of samyama); the

sixth of the eight limbs of yoga

DHARMA [dharma]
Duty or law

DHYANA [dhyāna]
Meditation (one of the three stages of samyama); the seventh of the eight limbs of yoga

GUNAS [guṇas]
Characteristic properties of matter

HRIDAYA [hṛdaya]
The heart

ISHVARA [īśvara]
The Supreme Being or Solar Logos

KAIVALYA [kaivalya]
Liberation; the state of perfect freedom

KARMA [karma]
Action, with reference to the law of cause and effect

KLESHA [kleśa]
A cause of sorrow or suffering

KRIYA [kriyā]
Preliminary, or practical (as of yoga)

MANAS [manas]
Mind principle

MANTRA [mantra]
A chant or invocation

NIRBIJA [nirbīja]
Without seed (as in meditation which has no object)

NIYAMA [niyama]
Fixed observance (the second of the eight limbs of yoga)

OM [om]
The Sacred Word or humming sound; designator of Ishvara

PARINAMA [pariṇāma]
  Transformation or change
PRAKRITI [prakṛti]
  Nature or matter; the phenomenal world; the Seen
PRANA [prāṇa]
  Vital force; breath or air
PRANAVA [praṇava]
  The humming sound OM; the designator of Ishvara
PRANAYAMA [prāṇāyāma]
  Control of the breath or vital energy; (the fourth of the
  eight limbs of yoga)
PRATYAHARA [pratyāhāra]
  Abstraction (the fifth of the eight limbs of yoga)
PRATYAYA [pratyaya]
  The content of the mind
PURUSHA [puruṣa]
  Soul; the indwelling consciousness; the Seer
RAJAS [rajas]
  Activity (one of the three gunas)
SABIJA [sabīja]
  With seed (as in meditation on an object)
SAMADHI [samādhi]
  Illumination; the state of wholeness; the final stage of the
  meditative process; (the last of the eight limbs of yoga)
SAMANA [samāna]
  One of the five airs or pranas which circulates in the region
  of the navel
SAMPRAJNATA [samprajñata]
  In full consciousness
SAMSKARA [saṃskāra]
  An impression (as may be left in the mind)

SAMYAMA [saṃyama]
  The three-fold meditation; the application of the last three limbs of yoga; perfect concentration of the mind

SATTVA [sattva]
  Equilibrium (one of the three gunas); the quality of goodness; the essence of matter

SIDDHI [siddhi]
  An occult power or psychic faculty

SUTRA [sūtra]
  A thread or aphorism (in philosophical use)

TAMAS [tamas]
  Inertia or inactivity (one of the three gunas)

UDANA [udāna]
  One of the five airs or pranas, relating to gravity

VAIRAGYA [vairāgya]
  Dispassion; desirelessness

YAMA [yama]
  Self-restraint (the first of the eight limbs of yoga)

YOGA [yoga]
  Union

INDEX

Roman numerals denote Books 1-4 followed by the sutra number; N. = Note; Q. = Question